SUMMER OLYMPIC LEGENDS

BASKETBALL

BY NATE LeBOUTILLIER

CREATIVE ● EDUCATION

BASKETBALL

CONTENTS

INTRODUCTION

Throughout human history, people have always sought to challenge themselves, to compete against others, and to discover the limits of their capabilities. Such desires can turn destructive, leading to war. But the ancient Greeks also recognized the good in these human traits, and it was because of them that the Olympic Games—featuring running races, jumping contests, throwing competitions, and wrestling and boxing matches—began more than 2,700 years ago. The ancient Olympics ended in A.D. 393, but the Games were revived in 1896 in hopes of promoting world peace through sports. Fittingly, the first "modern" Olympics were held in Athens, Greece, but they moved around the world every four years after that. In 2009, it was announced that the Games would be held in South America for the first time, going to Rio de Janeiro, Brazil, in 2016.

Every 1896 Olympian received a medal reading "International Olympic Games, Athens 1896"

Doctor James Naismith invented the game of basketball in Springfield, Massachusetts, in 1891. Thirteen years later, his sport was played for the first time as a demonstration at the third modern Olympics, which were held in 1904 in St. Louis, Missouri. In five contests, the Buffalo (New York) Germans swept the field, beating other American club teams from Chicago, San Francisco, New York, and St. Louis. Finally, in 1936 in Berlin, Germany, men's basketball was included as an official Olympic sport. Although the first tournament was held outdoors on courts built for tennis, 21 countries entered teams, with the United States coming out on top—starting a trend that would continue in the decades that followed. In 1976, women's basketball was contested at the Olympic level for the first time.

Although American athletes and teams long ruled the basketball courts of the Games, the sport has truly become international in recent decades. Players such as Oscar Schmidt of Brazil and Yao Ming of China—and countries ranging from the Soviet Union to Yugoslavia to Argentina—have enjoyed memorable moments of Olympic glory, if not always gold medals. Today, Dr. Naismith's game—with all its dazzling shots, fanciful passing, and inspiring teamwork—is one of the most popular and hotly contested of all the Olympic sports.

1896	1900	1904	1908	1912	1920	1924	1928	1932	1936	1948	1952	1956	1960	1964	1968	1972	1976	1980	1984	1988	1992	1996	2000	2004	2008	2012
ATHENS, GREECE	PARIS, FRANCE	ST. LOUIS, MISSOURI	LONDON, ENGLAND	STOCKHOLM, SWEDEN	ANTWERP, BELGIUM	PARIS, FRANCE	AMSTERDAM, NETHERLANDS	LOS ANGELES, CALIFORNIA	BERLIN, GERMANY	LONDON, ENGLAND	HELSINKI, FINLAND	MELBOURNE, AUSTRALIA	ROME, ITALY	TOKYO, JAPAN	MEXICO CITY, MEXICO	MUNICH, WEST GERMANY	MONTREAL, QUEBEC	MOSCOW, SOVIET UNION	LOS ANGELES, CALIFORNIA	SEOUL, SOUTH KOREA	BARCELONA, SPAIN	ATLANTA, GEORGIA	SYDNEY, AUSTRALIA	ATHENS, GREECE	BEIJING, CHINA	LONDON, ENGLAND

PLAYIN' IN THE RAIN

1936 BERLIN, GERMANY

The 1936 Games held in Berlin marked the first time basketball was played as an official Olympic sport. Twenty-one nations participated in that inaugural basketball tournament: Belgium, Brazil, Canada, Chile, China, Czechoslovakia, Egypt, Estonia, France, Germany, Italy, Japan, Latvia, Mexico, Peru, the Philippines, Poland, Switzerland, Turkey, the U.S., and Uruguay.

It was something of a revelation to many Americans that basketball was booming in countries besides the U.S. by 1936. But it soon became apparent that much of the world could play some serious hoops. In China, local amateur teams had long been entertaining crowds of more than 20,000 spectators, and Latvia had won the inaugural European Championship in basketball in 1935. At the Olympics, players from Japan and the Philippines garnered praise for their especially deft ball-handling and passing, and teams from Canada and Mexico were playing the game with impressive skill.

Still, the U.S. team was the cream of the crop in 1936. Led by two talented centers, Frank Lubin and Joe Fortenberry, the Americans set out for Europe by boat on a weeklong voyage that had them practicing their passing and dribbling on the ship's deck. Once the Americans got to Berlin, they quickly discovered that the Germans, led by dictator Adolf Hitler, had put little effort into running a world-class basketball tournament. "Hitler apparently didn't have [much of] a team," said Lubin, "and he didn't see fit to build a big basketball pavilion to house basketball because it wasn't important to them at that time. We played the games outdoors in rough

gravel, and the dust would get on our hands. It was very uncomfortable playing in this situation."

In fact, the basketball games in Berlin were played on modified tennis courts with limited room for spectators. The ball the Germans provided was of abnormal shape and inferior quality, and to make matters worse, the gold-medal game would end up being held during a rainstorm. To reach the gold-medal match, the U.S. defeated the Philippines and Mexico. Canada advanced by upending Uruguay and Poland. In the finals, with the court mostly underwater, the competition resembled water polo more than the game of basketball. "It was very slippery," Canadian guard Norm Dawson said of the court years later. "We couldn't execute any plays. When the ball hit the water it didn't move, so we simply passed the ball around." The U.S. prevailed in the soggy conditions by staking a 15–4 lead at halftime and then holding on for a 19–8 victory over its northern neighbors. Fittingly, James Naismith attended the 1936 Games and personally presented gold, silver, and bronze medals (which went to Mexico) to the winning teams.

Most spectators had to stand while watching Olympic basketball played under open skies in 1936

ATHENS, GREECE
PARIS, FRANCE
ST. LOUIS, MISSOURI
LONDON, ENGLAND
STOCKHOLM, SWEDEN
ANTWERP, BELGIUM
PARIS, FRANCE
AMSTERDAM, NETHERLANDS
LOS ANGELES, CALIFORNIA
BERLIN, GERMANY
LONDON, ENGLAND
HELSINKI, FINLAND
MELBOURNE, AUSTRALIA
ROME, ITALY
TOKYO, JAPAN
MEXICO CITY, MEXICO
MUNICH, WEST GERMANY
MONTREAL, QUEBEC
MOSCOW, SOVIET UNION
LOS ANGELES, CALIFORNIA
SEOUL, SOUTH KOREA
BARCELONA, SPAIN
ATLANTA, GEORGIA
SYDNEY, AUSTRALIA
ATHENS, GREECE
BEIJING, CHINA
LONDON, ENGLAND

1896
1900
1904
1908
1912
1920
1924
1928
1932
1936
1948
1952
1956
1960
1964
1968
1972
1976
1980
1984
1988
1992
1996
2000
2004
2008
2012

THE GRANDFATHER OF LITHUANIAN BASKETBALL

FRANK LUBIN U.S. POSITION: CENTER OLYMPIC COMPETITION: 1936

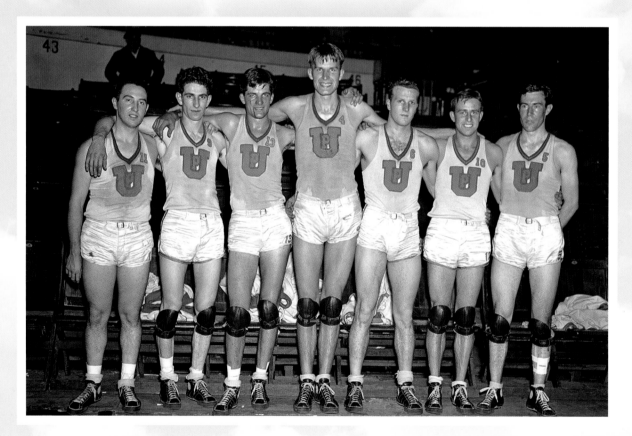

Frank Lubin was a tall basketball player for his time—nearly too tall. As a candidate for the first official U.S. Olympic basketball team that was to compete in the 1936 Games, Lubin, a 6-foot-6 center, wasn't even sure he'd be allowed to play due to his height. The world's official international

Frank Lubin (above, middle, and opposite, jumping) honed his skills playing for Universal Pictures

basketball organization, called FIBA (French for *Fédération Internationale de Basketball Amateur*), under pressure from many other competing countries, passed a rule shortly before the Games to limit the height of Olympic basketball players to 6-foot-1. That would have meant that Lubin and his 6-foot-8 teammate Joe Fortenberry would have been ineligible. Luckily for the Americans, better judgment prevailed, and the rule was revoked before play began.

Lubin, who grew up in Los Angeles after his parents emigrated from Lithuania, started playing basketball in high school after a particularly intense growth spurt left him six and a half feet tall. But it took a while for Lubin's coordination to catch up with his body. "My high school coach couldn't see any use for me," said Lubin. "He was making me jump center [for the tipoff] and then he'd put me on the bench." Soon, though, Lubin grew into his frame and became a star on the hardwood, playing collegiately at the University of California, Los Angeles (UCLA) before graduating in 1931. Later, Lubin took a job as a stagehand at the Universal Pictures movie studio and began playing basketball for their Amateur Athletic Union

(AAU) team. Universal had a fine team that took second place at the national AAU tournament in 1936. The first official U.S. men's Olympic basketball team was to be mostly made up of players from the tournament's top two teams, and thus Lubin was chosen. He helped the U.S. capture gold as the team's second-leading scorer in Berlin. Then, following the tournament, he decided to visit his father's homeland of Lithuania. Lubin ended up staying in Lithuania, off and on, for three years.

Lubin became so comfortable there that he began playing basketball with the locals and was eventually asked to train and coach Lithuanian athletes in the ways of American basketball. Lubin also starred for the Lithuanian national team that won European championships in 1937 and 1939. Many years later, disciples of Lubin competed for the Soviet Union (which won gold in 1972 and 1988) and Lithuania in subsequent Olympiads. "They're actually my second-generation students," said Lubin, who became known as "The Grandfather of Lithuanian Basketball." "I had no contact with the four boys that played for Russia in 1988, but my students coached in Lithuania for many years."

ATHENS, GREECE	PARIS, FRANCE	ST. LOUIS, MISSOURI	LONDON, ENGLAND	STOCKHOLM, SWEDEN	ANTWERP, BELGIUM	PARIS, FRANCE	AMSTERDAM, NETHERLANDS	LOS ANGELES, CALIFORNIA	BERLIN, GERMANY	LONDON, ENGLAND	HELSINKI, FINLAND	MELBOURNE, AUSTRALIA	**ROME, ITALY**	TOKYO, JAPAN	MEXICO CITY, MEXICO	MUNICH, WEST GERMANY	MONTREAL, QUEBEC	MOSCOW, SOVIET UNION	LOS ANGELES, CALIFORNIA	SEOUL, SOUTH KOREA	BARCELONA, SPAIN	ATLANTA, GEORGIA	SYDNEY, AUSTRALIA	ATHENS, GREECE	BEIJING, CHINA	LONDON, ENGLAND		
1896	1900	1904	1908	1912	1920	1924	1928	1932	1936	1948	1952	1956	**1960**	1964	1968	1972	1976	1980	1984	1988	1992	1996	2000	2004	2008	2012		

WHEN IN ROME…

1960 ROME, ITALY

The early years of Olympic basketball were glorious ones for the U.S., as American men captured gold in dominating fashion in one Olympiad after another. The squad that the U.S. fielded in 1960 might have been one of America's best amateur teams ever … in any sport. Headed by coach Pete Newell, "Team USA" included 6-foot-2 guard Jerry West, a superb team leader with pinpoint shooting accuracy;

The excellence of Oscar Robertson (right) and his 1960 teammates expanded basketball's global popularity

6-foot-5 guard Oscar Robertson, an impossibly athletic and versatile player; and 6-foot-8 forward Jerry Lucas, one of the most intelligent players to ever hit the hardwood.

Other nations arrived in Rome with their own prized players. Brazil was loaded with speedy guards, including Zenny de Azevedo, Carlos Domingos Massoni, and high scorers Wlamir Marques and Amaury Pasos. Italy boasted a pair of skilled shooters in 6-foot-3 Mario Alesini and 6-foot-4 Gianfranco Lombardi. The Soviet Union featured formidable big men Viktor Zubkov, a 6-foot-8 marvel of physical dexterity, and 7-foot-4 giant Ivan Krumminch, a former lumberjack who had quickly picked up the game of basketball after first trying it out at age 24. The Soviets were considered America's main competition, coming off a victory in 1958 over the Americans in the World Championships of Basketball. "The contests between the Soviet and U.S. teams were like a struggle between equals," said Soviet coach Stepan Spandarian. "The decisive advantage that the Americans once had no longer exists." Truly ramping up the rivalry was the fact that the U.S. and the Soviet Union were engaged in the Cold War, with political tensions between the countries ever rising.

Olympic officials instituted some new rules for Rome's 1960 basketball competition, most notably a trapezoidal lane—which limited the amount of time big men could camp out in the shadow of the basket—and a pool play format. Even the ball used in the 1960 Olympics was different. "You had to use whatever ball they played with in that country, and this one was really strange," said Coach Newell. "It was basically an 18-piece ball that had no pebble on it, and it was smaller than the ones we were used to." Newell went on to say that, though the ball seemed to have even a different weight to it, his players made do with it after watching Robertson take up the practice of "banking" the ball off the backboard and into the hoop and then following his lead.

Thanks to 17-points-per-game scoring averages by both Robertson and Lucas, the U.S. went undefeated in all 8 of its contests, including a convincing 81–57 victory over the silver medalist Soviets. Robertson, who would go on to become a huge star in the National Basketball Association (NBA), later recalled the pride he felt in accepting the gold medal, saying, "It was a moment of jubilation for me, a very special moment."

The U.S. squad was head and shoulders above the competition in 1960, averaging 102 points a game

A MUDDLED MESS
IN MUNICH

1972 MUNICH, WEST GERMANY

With fewer than 10 seconds remaining in the gold-medal game of the 1972 Olympic basketball tournament and the Soviet Union leading the U.S. 49–48, American guard Doug Collins snatched

Despite twice celebrating apparent victory, U.S. basketball endured its most bitter loss in the 1972 Games

an errant Soviet pass at midcourt and headed for the American basket from the left side. On Collins's hard-driving layup attempt, however, he was fouled and went flying headfirst to the hardwood where the floor met the basket support. Trainers rushed to Collins's aid, and Collins himself later reported that he had been briefly knocked unconscious, but the guard gathered himself and toed the free-throw line for two shots with just three seconds remaining on the clock. Collins coolly sank both shots, and the Americans gained the lead, 50–49.

Immediately following Collins's second free throw, the Soviets inbounded the ball, and the final seconds ticked off. The Americans began celebrating the victory. But the game's two referees, Brazilian Renato Righetto and Bulgarian Artenik Arabadjian, blew their whistles and huddled at the scorer's table with West German scorekeeper Hans Tenschert and Englishman R. William Jones, FIBA's secretary general, who had inexplicably come down out of the stands. The group began to discuss something, as much as individuals speaking different languages amid chaos can carry out a discussion. It seemed the officials were uncertain if the clock had been running properly, and there was some question as to whether the Soviet coaches had called a timeout.

As a result of the brief conference, three seconds were put back on the clock, and the Soviets were allowed to re-inbound the ball. This time, a full-court pass was deflected by the Americans, time elapsed, and the U.S. players again commenced celebrating having captured gold. But, again, the referees huddled at the scorer's table and decided that a clock error had occurred and that the Soviets should be given yet another try, again with three seconds remaining. On the Soviets' third attempt, they completed a full-court pass to their star forward, Alexander Belov, right under the hoop, and Belov simply laid the ball in the basket. Television replays showed the Soviet inbounder stepping over the line to throw the pass and Belov roughly jockeying for position with American forwards Jim Forbes (who ended up on the floor) and Kevin Joyce (who ended up out of bounds). But the referees called no

The U.S. has never accepted the 1972 basketball silver medals. They still sit unclaimed in a vault in Switzerland.

violation, and with Belov's basket, the Soviet Union had won the game, 51–50, and broken the Americans' 63-game Olympic basketball winning streak to capture the gold medal.

The U.S. protested the outcome, but an Olympic committee voted 3–2 to uphold the Soviets' win. Reactions to the bizarre controversy were fierce and varied. The U.S. team refused to accept its silver medals. Soviet coach Vladimir Kondrashkin said, "We deserve the victory no matter what the circumstances. We had them puzzled from the start since we used a different lineup to confuse them at the beginning." Righetto refused to sign the official scorebook as an indication that he thought that the game's ending was improper, and Tenschert maintained, "Under FIBA rules, the United States won."

U.S. players reacted to the shocking conclusion to the 1972 gold-medal game with confusion and anger

ATHENS, GREECE
PARIS, FRANCE
ST. LOUIS, MISSOURI
LONDON, ENGLAND
STOCKHOLM, SWEDEN
ANTWERP, BELGIUM
PARIS, FRANCE
AMSTERDAM, NETHERLANDS
LOS ANGELES, CALIFORNIA
BERLIN, GERMANY
LONDON, ENGLAND
HELSINKI, FINLAND
MELBOURNE, AUSTRALIA
ROME, ITALY
TOKYO, JAPAN
MEXICO CITY, MEXICO
MUNICH, WEST GERMANY
MONTREAL, QUEBEC
MOSCOW, SOVIET UNION
LOS ANGELES, CALIFORNIA
SEOUL, SOUTH KOREA
BARCELONA, SPAIN
ATLANTA, GEORGIA
SYDNEY, AUSTRALIA
ATHENS, GREECE
BEIJING, CHINA
LONDON, ENGLAND

1896 1900 1904 1908 1912 1920 1924 1928 1932 1936 1948 1952 1956 1960 1964 1968 1972 1976 1980 1984 1988 1992 1996 2000 2004 2008 2012

THE GENERAL TAKES CHARGE

1984 LOS ANGELES, CALIFORNIA

The 1984 Olympiad was an especially important one for the U.S. It was held on America's home turf in Los Angeles, and it marked America's return to Olympic action after a U.S. Olympic boycott of the 1980 Games in Moscow—an act of protest against Soviet military actions. When Bobby Knight was named coach of the 1984 U.S. basketball squad, it was clear that the U.S. was taking a

As a collegiate head coach from 1965 to 2008, Bobby Knight compiled an incredible 902 victories

no-nonsense approach. Knight, who coached a collegiate powerhouse at Indiana University, demanded near perfection from his players and berated them loudly if they didn't achieve it—a fiery leadership style that had earned him the nickname "The General."

The U.S. had an especially talented crop of collegians that year from which Knight could form his squad. There was athletic guard Michael Jordan from the University of North Carolina, towering center Patrick Ewing from Georgetown University, and sharpshooting forward Chris Mullin from St. John's University. But no other player at the time—not even Jordan, who would go on to become arguably the best player ever by way of an epic NBA career—stood out in 1984 like Auburn University forward Charles Barkley, a 6-foot-6 and 260-pound force of nature who could dribble the length of the floor for a rim-shaking dunk on one possession, sky for a rebound the next, and hip-check an opponent into the stands on the third.

The U.S. Olympic basketball trials were held in Bloomington, Indiana, under the watchful eye of Coach Knight, where Barkley proved he was perhaps the best player there. "Barkley's been dominant," said University of Michigan center Tim McCormick. "Three or four times a day, you see the backboard shaking. You look back and you see Barkley walking away." But Barkley's face could not hide his emotions, and his mouth never filtered any of his often controversial comments, opinions, or jokes. A long-lasting relationship between the free-spirited Barkley and the controlling Knight never had a chance, and after a couple of exhibitions at the Indianapolis Hoosier Dome that attracted in excess of 67,000 fans—then the largest crowd ever for any basketball game—Knight cut Barkley from the Olympic squad.

Fierce defense helped propel young guard Michael Jordan (right) and the U.S. to gold in 1984

The General took the players who made his cut and set them to the work of capturing gold in Los Angeles. Jordan, Ewing, Mullin, and young guard Steve Alford from Knight's own Indiana team were the four top scorers on a cohesive team that trounced the competition by an average of 32 points per game. Before the gold-medal matchup, Knight was set to prepare his team for battle with a fiery pep talk. But just before unleashing his speech, Knight discovered a note that Jordan had written on the back of a lockeroom chalkboard that said, in effect, "There's no way we lose this game after what you've put us through." Knight turned his players loose. The U.S. went out and dispatched Spain 96–65 to conclude the last Olympic basketball competition in which the U.S. would win gold with amateur athletes.

Several 1984 U.S. stars would return to the Olympics eight years later as part of the famed "Dream Team"

ATHENS, GREECE	PARIS, FRANCE	ST. LOUIS, MISSOURI	LONDON, ENGLAND	STOCKHOLM, SWEDEN	ANTWERP, BELGIUM	PARIS, FRANCE	AMSTERDAM, NETHERLANDS	LOS ANGELES, CALIFORNIA	BERLIN, GERMANY	LONDON, ENGLAND	HELSINKI, FINLAND	MELBOURNE, AUSTRALIA	ROME, ITALY	TOKYO, JAPAN	MEXICO CITY, MEXICO	MUNICH, WEST GERMANY	MONTREAL, QUEBEC	MOSCOW, SOVIET UNION	LOS ANGELES, CALIFORNIA	SEOUL, SOUTH KOREA	BARCELONA, SPAIN	ATLANTA, GEORGIA	SYDNEY, AUSTRALIA	ATHENS, GREECE	BEIJING, CHINA	LONDON, ENGLAND
1896	1900	1904	1908	1912	1920	1924	1928	1932	1936	1948	1952	1956	1960	1964	1968	1972	1976	1980	1984	1988	1992	1996	2000	2004	2008	2012

THE BRAZILIAN BOMBER

OSCAR SCHMIDT BRAZIL POSITION: FORWARD

OLYMPIC COMPETITIONS: 1980, 1984, 1988, 1992, 1996

Oscar Schmidt was the greatest scorer in Olympic men's basketball history. Nicknamed "Maõ Santa," Portuguese for "Holy Hand," and known simply as "Oscar" in his homeland, Schmidt, a 6-foot-9 forward with a lethal outside shot, starred for Brazil in an impressive five Olympiads from

Oscar Schmidt once made 90 straight free throws while playing games in a professional Brazilian league

1980 to 1996. In his Olympic basketball career, Schmidt played 38 games and scored a record 1,093 points for an average of 28.8 per game.

Brazil had its best team and best chance for an Olympic basketball medal with the 30-year-old Schmidt in his prime at the 1988 Games in Seoul, South Korea. In group play, Brazil opened with a pair of wins over Canada and China, with Schmidt scoring 36 and 44 points. Next up for Brazil was the vaunted U.S. team, which had a roster similar to the one Schmidt and his Brazilian teammates had defeated 120–115 the year before in the Pan American Games. In that contest, Schmidt had gone off for 46 points, including 35 in the second half alone, in a performance that was considered the greatest of his career. But at the 1988 Olympics, the Americans focused on containing Schmidt, who scored "just" 31, and the U.S. topped Brazil 102–87. Brazil rebounded to crush Egypt, with Schmidt scoring 39 points. He then tallied an amazing 55 points—an Olympic basketball single-game record—in a loss to Spain. Although Brazil lost 110–105 in the quarterfinals versus a heavily favored Soviet Union squad, Schmidt scored 46 points, and then had another 46 points in a fifth-place game victory over Puerto Rico, finishing with an incredible 42.4-points-per-game average for the 1988 Olympics.

In 1992, when the Olympics went to Barcelona, Spain, Schmidt again led all Olympic basketball scorers, this time with an average of 25 points per game. At the 1992 Olympiad, a reporter asked Schmidt if he considered it fair that he took most of the shots for Brazil, while his teammates were relegated to setting screens for him, passing him the ball, and playing defense, decidedly less glamorous aspects of the game. "Some people, they play the piano," said Schmidt. "And some people, they move the piano." When the U.S. "Dream Team" encountered Schmidt, American forward Scottie Pippen, a defensive stalwart, took special pride in limiting Schmidt to just 8-for-25 shooting as the U.S. set an Olympic scoring record in shellacking Brazil 127–83. But the resilient Schmidt returned one last time to play for Brazil in the 1996 Olympics, leading all scorers for a final time—even at the age of 38—with a robust 27.3-points-per-game average.

> **"Some people, they play the piano. And some people, they move the piano."** – Oscar Schmidt

Schmidt reminded many fans of American star Larry Bird, as both were crafty, 6-foot-9 sharpshooters

ATHENS, GREECE · PARIS, FRANCE · ST. LOUIS, MISSOURI · LONDON, ENGLAND · STOCKHOLM, SWEDEN · ANTWERP, BELGIUM · PARIS, FRANCE · AMSTERDAM, NETHERLANDS · LOS ANGELES, CALIFORNIA · BERLIN, GERMANY · LONDON, ENGLAND · HELSINKI, FINLAND · MELBOURNE, AUSTRALIA · ROME, ITALY · TOKYO, JAPAN · MEXICO CITY, MEXICO · MUNICH, WEST GERMANY · MONTREAL, QUEBEC · MOSCOW, SOVIET UNION · LOS ANGELES, CALIFORNIA · **SEOUL, SOUTH KOREA** · **BARCELONA, SPAIN** · ATLANTA, GEORGIA · SYDNEY, AUSTRALIA · ATHENS, GREECE · BEIJING, CHINA · LONDON, ENGLAND

1896 · 1900 · 1904 · 1908 · 1912 · 1920 · 1924 · 1928 · 1932 · 1936 · 1948 · 1952 · 1956 · 1960 · 1964 · 1968 · 1972 · 1976 · 1980 · 1984 · **1988** · **1992** · 1996 · 2000 · 2004 · 2008 · 2012

A SAD SPLIT

1988, 1992   SEOUL, SOUTH KOREA; BARCELONA, SPAIN

At the 1988 Olympics in Seoul, a young group of skilled Yugoslavians won six basketball games in blowout fashion and went on to take the silver medal. Those players—the most talented of them being Toni Kukoc, Dino Radja, Drazen Petrovic, Zarko Paspalj, and Vlade Divac—surprised many in Seoul with their great chemistry and creative play, but they were already well known in Europe. Thanks to Yugoslavia's disciplined national basketball organization, the group had been able to develop such teamwork by playing together since their early teenage years.

Kukoc, a silky-smooth ball handler and passer, was a 6-foot-11 swingman whose size belied his guard-like skills. Radja was a hardworking, 6-foot-10 power forward who could rebound and score inside

Dino Radja (above, left) and his countrymen (opposite) became a basketball power in the late 1980s

at a rapid pace. The 6-foot-5 Petrovic was a tireless worker and amazing shooter from long range as well as a fearless penetrator and usually the team's highest scorer. Paspalj was a sinewy, 6-foot-8 forward who shot with a left-handed, sidewinding motion that was unorthodox but deadly. And the 7-foot-1 Divac was a fun-loving, sure-handed big man who could dribble the length of the floor as easily as he could sink a hook shot.

In the 1990 FIBA World Basketball Championship, Yugoslavia zoomed past the U.S. and then whipped the Soviet Union in the final game, 92–75. "That was the point we thought Yugoslavian basketball could dominate the world," Kukoc later said. "The whole crowd stood up for us in a huge standing ovation. That was a huge thing for us, for our country."

Unfortunately, that game has been remembered more for an incident on the court during the postgame celebration in which Divac seized a fan's Croatian flag and threw it off the court. At that time, Yugoslavia was made up of the six republics of Croatia, Serbia, Slovenia, Montenegro, Macedonia, and Bosnia-Herzegovina. But tensions had recently begun

to rise between Croatia and Serbia, and because Kukoc, Radja, and Petrovic were from Croatia, while Paspalj and Divac were from Serbia, Divac's act also raised tensions within the team. "My reaction wasn't meant to show that I was against somebody," said Divac. "I just wanted to protect my team and show that we are a team from Yugoslavia, not from Croatia or Serbia or any other republic."

In 1991, war began to ravage parts of the formerly unified state. As a result, in the 1992 Olympics, Croatia fielded its own national basketball team that starred Kukoc, Petrovic, and Radja. Divac and Paspalj were forced to sit out, since Yugoslavia was banned by the International Olympic Committee (IOC). Watching Croatia— led by the scoring of Petrovic, who would tragically die in a car crash one year later—lose to America's famed Dream Team lineup in the gold-medal matchup sparked strong emotions in Divac. "I watched the game, but it wasn't easy," Divac said. "The silver medal was a great accomplishment for Croatia, but I always wonder what would have happened if my former teammates and I would have played together."

ATHENS, GREECE 1896

PARIS, FRANCE 1900

ST. LOUIS, MISSOURI 1904

LONDON, ENGLAND 1908

STOCKHOLM, SWEDEN 1912

ANTWERP, BELGIUM 1920

PARIS, FRANCE 1924

AMSTERDAM, NETHERLANDS 1928

LOS ANGELES, CALIFORNIA 1932

BERLIN, GERMANY 1936

LONDON, ENGLAND 1948

HELSINKI, FINLAND 1952

MELBOURNE, AUSTRALIA 1956

ROME, ITALY 1960

TOKYO, JAPAN 1964

MEXICO CITY, MEXICO 1968

MUNICH, WEST GERMANY 1972

MONTREAL, QUEBEC 1976

MOSCOW, SOVIET UNION 1980

LOS ANGELES, CALIFORNIA 1984

SEOUL, SOUTH KOREA 1988

BARCELONA, SPAIN 1992

ATLANTA, GEORGIA 1996

SYDNEY, AUSTRALIA 2000

ATHENS, GREECE 2004

BEIJING, CHINA 2008

LONDON, ENGLAND 2012

THE STARS (AND STRIPES) ALIGN

1992 BARCELONA, SPAIN

Michael Jordan. Magic Johnson. Larry Bird. They were three of the best and most influential basketball players who ever lived. They were also teammates on America's groundbreaking 1992

Legendary guard Magic Johnson won championships at the college, NBA, and Olympic levels

27

Olympic basketball team. Besides Jordan, Johnson, and Bird, the U.S. roster included guards John Stockton and Clyde Drexler, centers David Robinson and Patrick Ewing, and forwards Charles Barkley, Karl Malone, Scottie Pippen, Chris Mullin, and Christian Laettner. This superstar-laden squad became known simply as the Dream Team.

The U.S. was able to field such a formidable team for the 1992 Olympics in Barcelona because it was the first Olympiad at which FIBA allowed professional players to compete (even though, many contend, nations other than the U.S. had been circumventing this rule for years by allowing their "club" stars to compete in the Olympics). Many American players, coaches, and fans had been lobbying for the U.S. to throw its pro players into Olympic competition for some time—especially after the U.S. was thumped in the quarterfinals of the 1988 Olympics in Seoul

and ended up with the bronze medal instead of the usual gold.

When the Olympics began in Barcelona and the U.S. men's basketball team appeared at the opening ceremonies, it was apparent that the Dream Team would be treated like rock stars, complete with fans fawning over their every move. Even some opposing competitors took the opportunity to collect a little memorabilia—while playing against the Dream Team. During the Dream Team's Olympic debut, a 116–48 romp over Angola, Angolan players allegedly posed for pictures while the ball was in play. Although the Americans clearly enjoyed the spotlight and the chance to play with such talented teammates, they took their Olympic opportunity seriously.

Next up, the U.S. breezed past Croatia 103–70, then walloped Germany, Brazil, and Spain. America's wins were so decisive that it seemed the medal round would be a mere formality. It

Highflying guard Michael Jordan averaged almost 15 points a game for the Dream Team

was. Puerto Rico, Lithuania, and Croatia (again) couldn't touch the Dream Team as the routs continued, and the team many considered the best ever won the gold. All told, the Dream Team outscored the competition by an average margin of 43.8 points per game. "You will see a team of professionals in the Olympics again," said U.S. head coach Chuck Daly, "but I don't think you'll see another team quite like this."

Most people consider the 1992 roster led by coach Chuck Daly (center) the greatest ever assembled

1896 ATHENS, GREECE
1900 PARIS, FRANCE
1904 ST. LOUIS, MISSOURI
1908 LONDON, ENGLAND
1912 STOCKHOLM, SWEDEN
1920 ANTWERP, BELGIUM
1924 PARIS, FRANCE
1928 AMSTERDAM, NETHERLANDS
1932 LOS ANGELES, CALIFORNIA
1936 BERLIN, GERMANY
1948 LONDON, ENGLAND
1952 HELSINKI, FINLAND
1956 MELBOURNE, AUSTRALIA
1960 ROME, ITALY
1964 TOKYO, JAPAN
1968 MEXICO CITY, MEXICO
1972 MUNICH, WEST GERMANY
1976 MONTREAL, QUEBEC
1980 MOSCOW, SOVIET UNION
1984 LOS ANGELES, CALIFORNIA
1988 SEOUL, SOUTH KOREA
1992 BARCELONA, SPAIN
1996 ATLANTA, GEORGIA
2000 SYDNEY, AUSTRALIA
2004 ATHENS, GREECE
2008 BEIJING, CHINA
2012 LONDON, ENGLAND

GOLDEN GIRLS

1996 ATLANTA, GEORGIA

Women's Olympic sports such as gymnastics, swimming, and track and field have drawn keen fan interest since the early part of the 20th century. But although women's basketball became an official Olympic sport at the 1976 Games in Montreal, its popularity didn't truly rise until the 1996 Games in Atlanta.

Center Lisa Leslie (left) played in the 1996, 2000, 2004, and 2008 Olympics, winning gold every time

A number of factors helped to bring women's Olympic basketball to the forefront in 1996. First, the 1996 Olympics produced a truly great women's champion: the U.S. team. Many dazzling stars represented the U.S. squad, including a stable of towering yet nimble centers in 6-foot-5 Lisa Leslie, 6-foot-4 Rebecca Lobo, 6-foot-4 Venus Lacey, and 6-foot-2 Katrina McClain; do-it-all forwards Sheryl Swoopes, Nikki McCray, Carla McGhee, and Katy Steding; and a collection of tireless guards that included Dawn Staley, Ruthie Bolton, Jennifer Azzi, and Teresa Edwards.

Second, the American women were hungry, having lost to the Unified Team (a collection of former Soviet republics) in the previous Olympiad. Prior to the 1996 Olympics, this collection of players played an exhausting schedule of more than 50 exhibition games—winning each one—under the stern watch of coach Tara VanDerveer and became as dominant a squad as any ever seen in women's basketball.

Third, the public perception of women's basketball compared with men's basketball had changed and, for at least one Olympiad, seemed to favor women. Although the American men's Dream Team juggernaut had charmed the world at the 1992 Olympics, by 1996, fans had seemingly tired of the U.S. men "bullying" the overmatched competition. They were ready for a fresh victor.

The American women breezed through the competition, winning all eight of their games, including the gold-medal finale over Brazil, a 111–87 victory. Leslie, who averaged a team-best 19.5 points per game, led the U.S. in scoring with 29 points in the championship matchup, and every single American player scored. "I can't believe we would come this far and not play our best game," said Coach VanDerveer afterward. "This was our best whole game."

The popularity of the U.S. women's basketball team had another payoff: it strengthened the fan base of the new women's pro league in America that began play in 1997, the Women's National Basketball Association (WNBA). "That momentum [from the Olympics] generated the strongest push we could have imagined going into the first season of the WNBA," said inaugural WNBA president Val Ackerman. "The top players of that national team had signed up with the WNBA, and we were able to take advantage of the goodwill associated with their name."

The women's basketball team contributed to America's 44 total gold medals in the Atlanta Games

1896 ATHENS, GREECE
1900 PARIS, FRANCE
1904 ST. LOUIS, MISSOURI
1908 LONDON, ENGLAND
1912 STOCKHOLM, SWEDEN
1920 ANTWERP, BELGIUM
1924 PARIS, FRANCE
1928 AMSTERDAM, NETHERLANDS
1932 LOS ANGELES, CALIFORNIA
1936 BERLIN, GERMANY
1948 LONDON, ENGLAND
1952 HELSINKI, FINLAND
1956 MELBOURNE, AUSTRALIA
1960 ROME, ITALY
1964 TOKYO, JAPAN
1968 MEXICO CITY, MEXICO
1972 MUNICH, WEST GERMANY
1976 MONTREAL, QUEBEC
1980 MOSCOW, SOVIET UNION
1984 LOS ANGELES, CALIFORNIA
1988 SEOUL, SOUTH KOREA
1992 BARCELONA, SPAIN
1996 ATLANTA, GEORGIA
2000 SYDNEY, AUSTRALIA
2004 ATHENS, GREECE
2008 BEIJING, CHINA
2012 LONDON, ENGLAND

AN ARGENTINEAN ASCENSION

2004 ATHENS, GREECE

Entering the 2004 Olympics, no athlete from the country of Argentina had won an Olympic gold medal since 1952, when Tranquilo Cappozzo and Eduardo Guerrero topped all other world competitors in men's

Led by star Manu Ginobili, Argentina's 2004 team used exceptional teamwork to claim Olympic glory

double sculls rowing. That changed when the 2004 Argentinean men's basketball team stunned the Olympic field to capture gold.

Argentina's basketball fans might have known that something special was brewing when their team thrilled them with an opening-round, 83–82 win over Serbia-Montenegro on a last-second, fadeaway shot by star forward Manu Ginobili. Since joining the San Antonio Spurs of the NBA in 2002 and immediately helping lead them to a league title, the 6-foot-6 star had been wowing opponents and fans alike. "He was just a young skinny guy who looked like a winner," said Spurs coach Gregg Popovich about his first impression of Ginobili. "We didn't know he was going to be this good."

Although Ginobili was the only Argentinean player on an NBA roster at the time, others on the 2004 Olympic basketball team would soon enter the NBA, including inside players Fabricio Oberto and Luis Scola, forward Andres Nocioni, and guard Carlos Delfino. In addition to those talented players, point guard Pepe Sanchez had spent limited time in the NBA from 2000 to 2003, when he became the first Argentinean to play in the league. But talent alone wasn't what made Argentina championship-caliber. It was the way the team played together—the result of many members having been teammates for more than a decade—that set the squad apart.

The U.S. found this out firsthand in a semifinals loss to Argentina. The U.S., which had entered the 2004 Games with a cumulative Olympic basketball record of 109–2, had struggled in Athens, losing games to Puerto Rico and Lithuania in pool play, but many nonetheless considered the Americans favorites to win gold despite having left some of their greatest players (Shaquille O'Neal, Kevin Garnett, Kobe Bryant, Ray Allen, and Jason Kidd, among others) at home due to fears about security in Athens or scheduling conflicts. Argentina would not be denied, though, beating the U.S. 89–81. Ginobili proved unstoppable, scoring 29 points. "In 1992, the USA had the best players ever," Ginobili said after the win. "Here they are great players, too,

> **"The most special thing you can do is win for your country. We win in soccer in the morning and then in basketball. Argentina is on top of the world...."**
>
> – Manu Ginobili

but they are young and they never played internationally, so with different rules it's a whole different thing. The rest of the world is getting better, and the States isn't bringing their best players."

On August 28, 2004, Ginobili and his teammates brought home Argentina's first gold medal in 52 years by way of an 84–69 victory over Italy. To double their joy, Argentinean fans that same day watched their soccer team also win gold with a 1–0 victory over Paraguay.

Argentina lost two of its five preliminary games in 2004 but then streaked to gold with three wins

ATHENS, GREECE | PARIS, FRANCE | ST. LOUIS, MISSOURI | LONDON, ENGLAND | STOCKHOLM, SWEDEN | ANTWERP, BELGIUM | PARIS, FRANCE | AMSTERDAM, NETHERLANDS | LOS ANGELES, CALIFORNIA | BERLIN, GERMANY | LONDON, ENGLAND | HELSINKI, FINLAND | MELBOURNE, AUSTRALIA | ROME, ITALY | TOKYO, JAPAN | MEXICO CITY, MEXICO | MUNICH, WEST GERMANY | MONTREAL, QUEBEC | MOSCOW, SOVIET UNION | LOS ANGELES, CALIFORNIA | SEOUL, SOUTH KOREA | BARCELONA, SPAIN | ATLANTA, GEORGIA | SYDNEY, AUSTRALIA | ATHENS, GREECE | **BEIJING, CHINA** | LONDON, ENGLAND

1896 | 1900 | 1904 | 1908 | 1912 | 1920 | 1924 | 1928 | 1932 | 1936 | 1948 | 1952 | 1956 | 1960 | 1964 | 1968 | 1972 | 1976 | 1980 | 1984 | 1988 | 1992 | 1996 | 2000 | 2004 | **2008** | 2012

GOLDEN GLEAM REDEEMED

2008 BEIJING, CHINA

After the U.S. men's Olympic basketball team finished with the bronze medal in the 2004 Olympics, it went into the 2008 Games with something to prove. With that in mind, USA Basketball director Jerry Colangelo hired legendary Duke University coach Mike Krzyzewski to coach the team. Krzyzewski had played point guard for Army in the late 1960s. After college, Krzyzewski served five years in the U.S. Army and then went on to coach Duke to four national championships. "He was my pick because I thought he was the right guy for what we were trying to accomplish," said Colangelo. "He bleeds red, white, and blue, and he was as passionate as I was about what needed to be done."

Krzyzewski and Colangelo's efforts to help America reclaim gold started with assembling a cohesive team that featured sharp shooting, defensive prowess, and unbeatable bench depth. And after America's

By 2008, many countries were sending players with NBA experience to represent them in the Games

disappointing finish in 2004, it seemed more of the NBA's biggest stars were willing to take up the challenge, including versatile forward LeBron James and high-scoring guards Kobe Bryant and Dwyane Wade.

In basketball-crazy China, the U.S. stars were a hit, eliciting adulation wherever they went, which included sightseeing trips to local attractions and attendance at their fellow U.S. Olympians' competitions. To open the tournament, "Redeem Team," as the U.S. squad was nicknamed, topped host China by 31 points in a game that drew enormous worldwide interest. The Americans then proceeded to pound Angola, Greece, Spain, and Germany in group play. In the elimination portion of the tournament, the U.S. whipped Australia 116–85 and then faced Argentina, the team that won Olympic gold in 2004 behind NBA star Manu Ginobili. Unfortunately for Argentina, Ginobili suffered an ankle injury in the game's opening minutes and had to watch as the U.S. routed his countrymen, 101–81.

For the gold, the U.S. met Spain for a second time. The game was a high-scoring affair with the U.S. constantly threatening to pull away, but Spain—which featured towering brothers Pau and Marc Gasol inside and a wily pack of backcourt players in Rudy Fernandez, Juan Carlos Navarro, and teenage sensation Ricky Rubio—continually made inspired counter-runs. With the game winding down, Bryant and Wade both hit big three-pointers to secure a 118–107 victory and the gold medal for the U.S. "We played with great character in one of the great games in international basketball history," said Krzyzewski following the contest. "Spain was fabulous. We couldn't stop them completely. Everyone played at the highest level, and it brought out the best in us, and we're ecstatic, just ecstatic."

By the conclusion of the 2008 Games, U.S. men's basketball teams had medaled at every Olympics at which they had competed, winning 13 gold medals, 1 silver, and 2 bronze. Overall, the American men carried a 122–5 record, going 35–3 in games in which U.S. teams featured professional players from the NBA.

Kobe Bryant netted 20 points and notched 6 assists as the U.S. romped past Spain in the 2008 finals

The 2008 matchup between the U.S. and China was one of the most publicized events of the Beijing Games

1896	1900	1904	1908	1912	1920	1924	1928	1932	1936	1948	1952	1956	1960	1964	1968	1972	1976	1980	1984	1988	1992	1996	2000	2004	2008	2012
ATHENS, GREECE	PARIS, FRANCE	ST. LOUIS, MISSOURI	LONDON, ENGLAND	STOCKHOLM, SWEDEN	ANTWERP, BELGIUM	PARIS, FRANCE	AMSTERDAM, NETHERLANDS	LOS ANGELES, CALIFORNIA	BERLIN, GERMANY	LONDON, ENGLAND	HELSINKI, FINLAND	MELBOURNE, AUSTRALIA	ROME, ITALY	TOKYO, JAPAN	MEXICO CITY, MEXICO	MUNICH, WEST GERMANY	MONTREAL, QUEBEC	MOSCOW, SOVIET UNION	LOS ANGELES, CALIFORNIA	SEOUL, SOUTH KOREA	BARCELONA, SPAIN	ATLANTA, GEORGIA	**SYDNEY, AUSTRALIA**	**ATHENS, GREECE**	**BEIJING, CHINA**	LONDON, ENGLAND

HOMETOWN HERO

YAO MING CHINA POSITION: CENTER OLYMPIC COMPETITIONS: 2000, 2004, 2008

On August 9, 2008, more television viewers tuned in to watch a basketball game than ever had before. Some estimates put total viewership at up to 1 billion people. That evening, the U.S. was taking on China on its home floor at the Beijing Olympics. Former U.S. president George W. Bush was in attendance, as was Chinese foreign minister Yang Jiechi.

Not only unusually tall for a Chinese person, Yao Ming was among the tallest NBA players ever

As the players stretched and took the court—the Chinese in stark red with yellow and the Americans in white with navy and red—the crowd buzzed with claps and chants of *CHI-NA! CHI-NA!* "I've never felt an environment quite like this," said U.S. guard Kobe Bryant. "I've played in many big games, but the energy tonight was different."

The opening tip went to the U.S., but the Americans threw the ball away. China then inbounded the ball. After a pick and roll, Yao Ming received a pass at the top of the key, just behind the three-point line. Yao faced the goal and set his feet to shoot....

The 27-year-old Yao, a 7-foot-6 center, was China's best player and the idol of millions of basketball players across China. Born in Shanghai in 1980 to parents who had both played for Chinese Olympic teams, Yao learned basketball early and was playing for his hometown club, the Shanghai Sharks, by age 16. As his coach said, "We had been looking forward to the arrival of Yao Ming for three generations." Yao's incredible combination of extreme height, light shooting touch, defensive tenacity, and selfless attitude was truly groundbreaking. In 2002, the Houston Rockets won the first pick in the NBA Draft Lottery and negotiated Yao's release from the

Sharks in order to make him the first foreign-born top pick in the history of the Draft. Yao rewarded the Rockets with his fine play and won over millions of new American fans during the next five seasons. But for many Chinese, Yao's first and foremost duty was not to gain personal glory but to dominantly represent his homeland. For this reason, the Olympics of 2008—the first Games to be held in China—were utterly important to the career of Yao Ming.

As Yao focused on the basket from behind the three-point line in Beijing, the fact that he had made only one three-pointer in his NBA career up to that point might have fluttered through his mind. Regardless, the big center raised the ball over his head, his elbows jutting out, and launched the shot. Nearly a billion pairs of eyes watched the ball as it arced and splashed through the net. "He scripted it perfect," said U.S. guard Dwyane Wade. "You just had to smile because you couldn't write it any better."

The U.S. would go on to beat China 101–70, and Yao would finish the game shooting just 3-for-10 from the field. But for one moment, Yao Ming had sunk an enormous, game-opening shot, China was in the lead against the U.S., and any dream was possible on the courts of China.

1896	1900	1904	1908	1912	1920	1924	1928	1932	1936	1948	1952	1956	1960	1964	1968	1972	1976	1980	1984	1988	1992	1996	2000	2004	2008	**2012**
ATHENS, GREECE	PARIS, FRANCE	ST. LOUIS, MISSOURI	LONDON, ENGLAND	STOCKHOLM, SWEDEN	ANTWERP, BELGIUM	PARIS, FRANCE	AMSTERDAM, NETHERLANDS	LOS ANGELES, CALIFORNIA	BERLIN, GERMANY	LONDON, ENGLAND	HELSINKI, FINLAND	MELBOURNE, AUSTRALIA	ROME, ITALY	TOKYO, JAPAN	MEXICO CITY, MEXICO	MUNICH, WEST GERMANY	MONTREAL, QUEBEC	MOSCOW, SOVIET UNION	LOS ANGELES, CALIFORNIA	SEOUL, SOUTH KOREA	BARCELONA, SPAIN	ATLANTA, GEORGIA	SYDNEY, AUSTRALIA	ATHENS, GREECE	BEIJING, CHINA	**LONDON, ENGLAND**

THE GAMES OF 2012

The 2012 Olympics were to be held in London, England. Londoners got the news in July 2005, and as is the case any time an Olympic host is selected, city and national officials sprang into action. Although seven years may seem to be plenty of time for preparation, it is in fact a small window when one considers that host cities typically need to create housing for thousands of

In 2012, London was to play host to its third Summer Olympiad, having done so in 1908 and 1948

international athletes and coaches (generally in a consolidated area known as the "Athletes' Village"), expand public transportation options (such as trains and buses), and build outdoor playing fields, indoor arenas, and other venues with enough seating—and grandeur—to be worthy of Olympic competition.

The numbers involved in the 2012 Games indicate just how large a venture it is to host an Olympiad. Some 10,500 athletes from 200 countries were to compete in London, with 2,100 medals awarded. About 8 million tickets were expected to be sold for the Games. And before any athletes arrived or any medals were awarded, it was anticipated that the total cost of London's Olympics-related building projects and other preparations would approach $15 billion.

Among those construction projects was the creation of Olympic Park, a sprawling gathering area in east London that was to function as a center of activity during the Games. From the park, people would be able to move to numerous athletic facilities in and around the city. Those facilities included the 80,000-seat Olympic Stadium, which was built to host track

and field events as well as the opening and closing ceremonies; the new Basketball Arena, a temporary structure that was to be dismantled after the Games; and the $442-million Aquatics Centre, which was designed both to host swimming events and to serve as a kind of visitors' gateway to Olympic Park. Other notable venues included the North Greenwich Arena (which was to host gymnastics), the ExCeL center (boxing), Earls Court (indoor volleyball), and Horse Guards Parade (beach volleyball).

In July 2011, British prime minister David Cameron and IOC president Jacques Rogge reviewed all preparations and proudly declared that the city was nearly ready to welcome the world. "This has the makings of a great British success story," Cameron announced. "With a year to go, it's on time, it's on budget.... We must offer the greatest ever Games in the world's greatest country."

Rogge kicked off the one-year countdown to the Games by formally inviting countries around the world to send their greatest athletes to the British capital in 2012. "The athletes will be ready," said Rogge. "And so will London."

amateur — not a professional; basketball players who compete professionally (for pay) were not allowed in Olympic competition until 1992

Amateur Athletic Union (AAU) — a U.S. sports organization formed in 1888 that oversees and promotes amateur sports and physical fitness

backcourt — describing the part of one-half a basketball court farthest away from the basket, or the players (primarily guards) who spend most of their time there

boycott — the act of protesting or showing disapproval of something by refusing to participate in an event

circumventing — going around something, often strategically and in a way that bends rules

club teams — teams that are organized and overseen by a private individual or company

Cold War — a prolonged rivalry between the Soviet Union and its communist supporters and the U.S. and its democratic allies; it lasted from the end of World War II until the collapse of the Soviet Union in 1991

disciples — people who learn from a leader such as a teacher or a coach and help to spread the lessons they learn

Draft Lottery — a lottery system used by the NBA to determine the order in which the league's worst teams get to choose among the most talented amateur players available in a given year

fadeaway — describing a basketball shot in which a player leaps backward as he or she shoots, thereby making the shot more difficult to block

group play — a tournament format in which athletes or teams are divided up into groups and play each other to determine which athletes or teams advance farther into the tournament

inbounded — passed the ball into play from out of bounds in order to resume game action

penetrator — a player with sufficient quickness and ball-handling skill to drive through a defense to the basket

pick and roll — an offensive basketball play in which a player screens for the dribbler (assumes a stationary position to block the opposing defender with his body), then moves, or "rolls," toward the basket in hopes of receiving a pass from the dribbler for an easy shot

pool play — a tournament format in which all athletes or teams play each other at least once, and failure to win a contest does not result in immediate elimination

powerhouse — a person, team, or group that has achieved great (and often steady) success or shows the potential to do so

screens — offensive basketball maneuvers in which a player without the ball assumes a stationary position that impedes the movement of an opposing team's player; also called picks

swingman — a basketball player who can play either the guard or forward positions; a swingman is usually relatively tall but with good quickness and ball-handling skill

unorthodox — describing a style or manner that differs from a generally approved or widely accepted style or manner

Selected Bibliography

Anderson, Dave. *The Story of the Olympics*. New York: HarperCollins, 2000.

Cunningham, Carson. *American Hoops: U.S. Men's Olympic Basketball from Berlin to Beijing*. Lincoln, Neb.: University of Nebraska Press, 2009.

Guttmann, Allen. *The Olympics: A History of the Modern Games*. Urbana: University of Illinois Press, 2002.

MacCambridge, Michael, ed. *SportsCentury*. New York: ESPN, 1999.

Macy, Sue, and Bob Costas. *Swifter, Higher, Stronger: A Photographic History of the Summer Olympics*. Washington, D.C.: National Geographic Books, 2008.

Maraniss, David. *Rome 1960: The Olympics That Changed the World*. New York: Simon & Schuster, 2008.

Sports Illustrated. "SI Vault: Your Link to Sports History." SI.com. http://sportsillustrated.cnn.com/vault.

USA Basketball. "The Official Site of USA Basketball." http://www.usabasketball.com.

Web Sites

International Olympic Committee
www.olympic.org
This site is the official online home of the Olympics and features profiles of athletes, overviews of every sport, coverage of preparation for the 2012 Summer Games, and more.

Sports-Reference / Olympic Sports
www.sports-reference.com/olympics
This site is a comprehensive database for Olympic sports and features complete facts and statistics from all Olympic Games, including medal counts, Olympic records, and more.

INDEX

Published by Creative Education
P.O. Box 227, Mankato, Minnesota 56002
Creative Education is an imprint of
The Creative Company
www.thecreativecompany.us

Design and production by The Design Lab
Art direction by Rita Marshall

Printed by Corporate Graphics in
the United States of America

Photographs by American Numismatic Society, Corbis (Bettmann), Dreamstime (Alain Lacroix), Getty Images (Allsport Hulton/Archive, Allsport UK /Allsport, Archive Photos, Andrew D. Bernstein/NBAE, Nathaniel S. Butler/NBAE, Rich Clarkson//Time Life Pictures, David Eulitt/Kansas City Star/MCT, Andy Hayt/Sports Illustrated, Jed Jacobsohn, Peter Read Miller /Sports Illustrated, Chris McGrath, FILIPPO MONTEFORTE/AFP, Doug Pensinger, Popperfoto, Mike Powell/ALLSPORT, ANTONIO SCORZA/AFP, Jamie Squire, Dusan Vranic/Pool, John G. Zimmerman /Sports Illustrated), iStockphoto (ray roper), Shutterstock (Sylvana Rega)

Library of Congress
Cataloging-in-Publication Data
LeBoutillier, Nate.
Basketball / by Nate LeBoutillier.
p. cm. — (Summer Olympic legends)
Summary: A survey of the highlights and legendary athletes—such as Brazilian Oscar Schmidt—of the Olympic sport of basketball, which officially became a part of the modern Summer Games in 1936.
Includes bibliographical references and index.
ISBN 978-1-60818-208-4
1. Basketball players—Biography—Juvenile literature. 2. Basketball—Juvenile literature. 3. Olympics—Juvenile literature. I. Title.
GV884.A1 L44 2012
796.323—dc23   2011032494

CPSIA: 030111 PO1452

First Edition
9 8 7 6 5 4 3 2 1